Red-Eared Sliders

FROM THE EXPERTS AT
ADVANCED VIVARIUM SYSTEMS™

By Philippe de Vosjoli

THE HERPETOCULTURAL LIBRARY™
Advanced Vivarium Systems™
Mission Viejo, California

Special thanks to Clive Longden and Dorothy De Lisle for their invaluable advice.

Jarad Krywicki, *editor*
Kristin Mehus-Roe, *project manager*
Nick Clemente, *special consultant*
Designed by Michael Vincent Capozzi
Suzy Gehrls, *production manager*
All photos by Philippe de Vosjoli except where otherwise indicated
Rachel Rice, *indexer*

LCCN: 96-183295

Cover photography by David Northcott

P.O. Box 6050
Mission Viejo, CA 92690
www.avsbooks.com
(877) 4-AVS-BOOK

We want to hear from you. What books would you like to see in the future? Please feel free to write us with any comments on our AVS books.

Printed in Singapore
10 9 8 7 6 5 4 3

CONTENTS

INTRODUCTION

Red-eared sliders and other freshwater turtles have been remarkably successful in colonizing freshwater habitats. In some areas, the density of these omnivorous predators is truly staggering. Their ability to survive and thrive in such areas is due, in part, to their relatively high intelligence and adaptive skills.

However, no matter how successful they are in the wild, they are ill prepared for the neglect and poor treatment often experienced in captivity at the hands of children. Ultimately, it is a parent's responsibility to ensure this neglect does not occur. Turtles are not cheap, living play toys or substitutes for Teenage Mutant Ninja Turtles. Red-eared sliders and other freshwater turtles need proper care, attention, and a captive environment that may cost a significant amount of money. Of the several million hatchling red-ears sold outside of the United States, nearly 90 percent die in the first year. A large percentage of the adults sold in the general pet trade also die within their first year following capture. Considering that they are relatively easy reptiles to raise in captivity, this is an abomination.

When kept properly, red-eared sliders and other freshwater turtles are attractive, interesting animals easily capable of delighting their owners. A well-designed vivarium (a reptile enclosure that simulates the animal's natural environment) can provide a display as eye-catching and fascinating as any tropical fish aquarium. In fact, several aspects of freshwater habitats can be successfully simulated in one's home. These simulations will unlock a world not readily accessible to most people.

This book provides all the necessary information for you to successfully keep, display, and breed red-eared sliders and other popular freshwater turtles. A number of exotic freshwater turtle species can be maintained under the same general guidelines, as long as the vivarium temperatures are adjusted to meet the requirements of the species.

CHAPTER 1
GENERAL INFORMATION

R ed-eared sliders belong to the large turtle family Emydidae. They are a subspecies of the large and variable *Trachemys scripta* complex, which currently consists of fourteen subspecies that inhabit the United States, Mexico, Central America, and parts of South America.

The current scientific name of red-eared sliders is *Trachemys scripta elegans*. In most older publications, red-eared sliders and their relatives are listed under the genera *Chrysemys* or *Pseudemys*.

Given a proper setup, red-eared sliders make one of the most stunning and interesting vivarium animals available. Photo by Bill Love

Distribution: Red-eared sliders range from Indiana to New Mexico and south to the Gulf of Mexico and extreme northeast Mexico. There are relict colonies in Ohio, West Virginia, and Kentucky. As a result of released or escaped captives, populations also exist in several other localities.

Size: Adults normally reach 5 to 8 inches long. The largest recorded red-eared slider measured 11 inches.

Sexing: Males are smaller than females. When mature, males develop long foreclaws and have longer tails with a thicker base than those of females. In males, the vent (opening to the cloaca, the common cavity in which genital, digestive, and urinary tracts release their contents) is located at a greater distance from the body than in females. Hatchlings cannot be reliably sexed.

Mature male red-eared sliders (left) have a significantly longer tail than females (right).

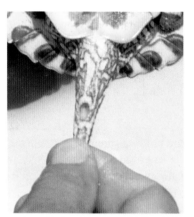

Mature male red-eared sliders (left) have more elongated foreclaws than females (right).

Growth: In males, sexual maturity is a function of size, reached at a length of 3 to 4 inches. Depending on care, they achieve this size in two to four years. For females, sexual maturity appears to depend on age, not size. In the wild, females become sexually mature between five and seven years old. Mature females usually have a shell length of at least 5 inches. When raised under optimal captive conditions without hibernation, males reach sexual maturity in two and a half years and females reach it in three and a half years. Hatchlings and young animals fed high protein diets (25 to 40 percent) have a faster growth rate. Once these animals reach sexual maturity, reduce the protein to 10 to 25 percent of their diet.

Longevity: If kept under the proper conditions, red-eared sliders often live for fifteen to twenty-five years, sometimes even longer.

Color and Color Morphs

Because several million red-eared sliders are produced annually for sale outside of the United States and because many hobbyists selectively breed color morphs for their aesthetic appeal, several color morphs of red-eared sliders are now available in the specialist reptile trade. The most popular morph is the albino red-eared slider, which, as a juvenile, is bright lemon yellow with prominent orange-red patches on the sides of the head. These albino red-ears vary in color intensity. Some have more washed out yellow coloration than others. As they grow into adults, the yellow tends to fade to cream yellow, but factors such as diet may affect this. Further selective breeding, such as outbreeding with ornate red-eared sliders from Texas, may improve this trait.

Most other red-eared slider morphs are sold under the general category "pastel." The term is applied to a wide variety of color morphs, characterized by varying degrees of hypomelanism (reduced black), hypoxanthism (reduced yellow), aberrations in pattern, and varying degrees of yellow and red pigmentation. Thus, one can have "high red" pastels or "high yellow" pastels. "Ghost" pastels, animals with an even grayish yellow coloration and no red or black pigmentation, are also available. Some pastel sliders have deep red eyes as a result of amelanism. Red-eared slider morphs have not been sufficiently clarified, and it may be several years before the many characteristics arbitrarily dumped under the pastel category are satisfactorily explained and isolated. Many pastel sliders have asymmetries and defects that suggest either incubation at inadequate temperatures or the expression of recessive genes. Examples include asymmetric shell patterns and/or scutes, reduced size of one or both eyes, and unusual enlargement of one or both eyes (often called "pop eye").

Crossed or unusually large eyes are common in pastel sliders, and may be due to inadequate incubation temperatures.

Some herpetoculturists (those who study and keep reptiles or amphibians) believe that many of the pastel traits are temperature induced and not necessarily of a genetic nature. Others assert that a significant percentage of pastel red-ears are of genetic origin because the category contains such a wide range of variant and aberrant turtles. Because of an increased interest in the selective breeding of red-eared sliders, it is likely that these issues will be clarified in the near future. In any case, considering the colorful nature of red-eared sliders, few turtles have such aesthetic potential for selective breeding.

Color Changes: Many populations of red-eared sliders

become more melanistic (an increased amount of black body and shell pigmentation) as they get older. This is particularly true in males, where the changes in pigmentation appear to be linked to the production of the male hormone testosterone, and thus tend to correlate with the

Albino red-eared sliders vary in color intensity.

This is an adult female albino red-eared slider. Photo by Chris Wood

Hatchling and juvenile albino red-eared sliders have a bright yellow coloration.

Note the absence of leg striping on this unusually attractive pastel red-eared slider.

This "high red pastel" slider has red on the top of the head as well as in the dorsal pattern.

growth of the foreclaws. As the animals age, their shell and various body parts may become suffused in black.

Variation: Although red-eared sliders are considered a single subspecies of *Trachemys scripta*, there is variation

These adult red-eared sliders clearly demonstrate the tendency towards melanism in older specimens.

among populations from different areas. As adults, typical red-eared sliders sold in the pet trade, which are primarily collected in Louisiana, bear relatively low contrast patterns on their shell and have dark background colors. On the other hand, red-eared sliders originating from parts of Texas, often sold as "ornate" red-eared sliders, have a bright yellow and orange shell background coloration and highly contrasting dark patterns.

"Ornate" red-eared sliders belong to the same subspecies as typical red-eared sliders, but they originate from a different part of the United States.

CHAPTER 2
BEFORE YOU BUY

The vast majority of hatchling sliders sold in the pet trade die of neglect or mistreatment. To avoid contributing to this problem, do not purchase a turtle if any of the following apply:

1) You are unwilling to take responsibility for the animal.

2) You plan to purchase the animal for children but are unwilling to supervise its care.

3) You have doubts about owning a turtle.

4) You cannot provide an adequate setup.

The absolute minimum setup requirements for a red-eared slider are:

Enclosure: Provide at least a 30-gallon aquarium or a large plastic container, such as a concrete mixing tub or a small kiddy pool.

Basking Site: Use a section of cork or smooth rock that the turtle can readily access. Place it under a reflector type light fixture with a 60-, 75-, or 100-watt bulb, depending on the temperature. Keep it on twelve to fourteen hours a day. If the temperature at night is less than 65 degrees Fahrenheit (F), leave the light on at night.

Aquarium Thermometer: Monitor the water temperature and measure the temperature of the basking site. The water should be 76-84° F. The basking site should measure 82-88° F.

Food: Feed turtles every one to two days. Suitable diets include pre-killed feeder guppies, very small floating goldfish pellets, small-grade trout chow, crushed reptile floating sticks, or low-fat, high-quality canned dog food. Place a small section of romaine or red leaf lettuce in the water for turtles to graze on.

Water: Change tank water every two days. It should be deep enough to cover the turtle's shell and can be considerably deeper if gradients are created with rocks leading to basking areas.

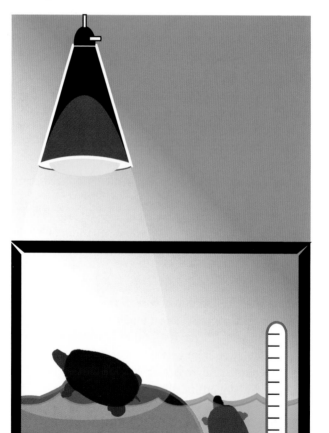

The most basic setup for raising red-eared sliders must at least consist of a large plastic container, a slab of cork bark or rock basking area, a reflector-type spotlight or desk lamp, and a thermometer.

CHAPTER 3

SELECTING A HEALTHY RED-EARED SLIDER

Your initial selection process is a critical factor to long-term success with a red-eared slider. To locate a suitable specimen:

1) Examine the dealer's turtles and their captive conditions. The water must be relatively clean, and the turtles must appear active and alert. Select an active and alert animal that appeals to you.

2) Pick up the turtle you want. The turtle should have good weight. You should not be surprised by how light it is. If the turtle is active in your hands, the movement of its limbs should be vigorous. Gently pull on one of its hind feet; the turtle should have a strong withdrawal response. Sick turtles are often light, and tend to be limp with weak withdrawal responses.

3) Look carefully at the head area. The eyes should appear open and clear. Avoid animals with swollen, shut, or clouded eyes. Look at the cheek areas; they should be smooth and equal in size when viewed from above. Avoid specimens whose heads are large or swollen on one side.

4) Examine the limbs and tail area to make sure that there are no injuries or unusual swellings.

5) Now, examine the shell. Look for injuries or signs of shell infection on the carapace (top part of the shell) and the plastron (bottom part of the shell). These infections look like irregular light or dark patches on or beneath the keratinous (superficial layer of shell that contains the insoluble protein called keratin) shell. While holding the turtle

in your hand, press lightly against the plastron. If it feels soft and flexible, do not purchase the turtle. A flexible shell or plastron is a sign of metabolic bone disease (see **Diseases and Disorders**). You can also check for metabolic bone disease by lightly pressing down on the rear marginals (back edge of the shell). Turtles with the disease will have flexible marginal scutes. If the symptoms are minimal, a turtle can be treated by correcting its diet with calcium and vitamin D$_3$ supplements.

This is a healthy two-year-old captive-raised red-eared slider. Photo by Chris Wood

CHAPTER 4

HOUSING AND GENERAL CARE

I f properly set up, a water turtle vivarium provides as much viewing pleasure as a tropical fish tank. Turtles move through water as effortlessly as fish, and they demonstrate many interesting behaviors, including a certain degree of responsiveness toward their owners. Unfortunately, many turtle buyers perceive red-eared sliders as inexpensive children's pets and are unwilling to spend the money required for proper maintenance, display, and appreciation of the animals. If you are unable or unwilling to purchase an aquarium-style enclosure, there are other alternatives that meet a turtle's basic needs.

This close-up of a young red-eared slider clearly displays the red patch found on the side of the head. Photo by Chris Estep

Basic Requirements

To keep water turtles in captivity, supply the following:

1) An enclosure large enough to hold an appropriate amount of water.

2) Clean water.

3) An area where turtles can leave the water to dry out and bask.

4) A heat source.

5) A proper diet.

6) Regular monitoring and maintenance of your animals and setup.

Enclosures

Several types of enclosures are suitable for freshwater turtles. The most attractive are all-glass aquaria, which allow owners to easily observe turtles swimming, climbing on basking areas, and exhibiting their many other behaviors. For one typical 4- to 5-inch-long red-eared slider, use at least a 30-gallon long aquarium, preferably something larger. If you are keeping two or more animals, figure at least 10 extra gallons per additional animal, as long as you use a standard size aquarium and not an unusually tall one. The surface area of your enclosure should measure about 2 square feet (minimum) for one turtle and an extra square foot for each additional turtle. For female red-eared sliders 8 inches or longer, double the requirements mentioned above. If in doubt, ask yourself whether you want to display your turtle in a prison or a playground. A turtle kept in a dishpan with shallow water behaves very differently than one provided with the space and water depth it needs to perform a wide range of normal behaviors.

If you don't care about viewing your turtle from the side, you can house your turtles in a variety of containers, including plastic tubs, cement mixing containers, and concrete, plastic, or fiberglass pools. Just don't use a small container; give the animal room to move. Do not use a dishpan or small plastic tub. With large ground-level pools, construct a barrier around it to prevent escape.

If you can't devote a large enclosure to your turtles,

don't buy a red-eared slider. There are other smaller species of turtles that can be maintained in smaller enclosures, such as musk, mud, or Reeve's turtles. Some exotic species, such as big-head turtles *(Platysternon megacephalum)*, also can be kept in smaller aquaria but, as a rule, turtles are best displayed in larger enclosures.

Large plastic containers, though not ideal, make acceptable enclosures for eastern painted turtles. A large slab of cork serves as a basking area for this eastern painted turtle.

This attractive aquarium setup is home to albino (right) and ornate red-eared sliders.

Basking Areas

Red-eared sliders and most other freshwater turtles require a basking or land area where they can emerge from the water and warm themselves under a heat source. The drying out of the skin and shell that occurs during basking is also beneficial. Basking areas can consist of islands and platforms established at the water line of the tank, or areas built from the bottom of the tank that emerge above water level. One of the best materials for basking areas is natural cork bark. It can be purchased or mail ordered from specialized reptile stores. The best types are thick, rounded slabs of cork bark, which provide some footing for turtles to climb. Natural cork bark simply floats on top of the water without significantly limiting the water volume of the enclosure. You can also wedge cork in a fixed position between two sides of an aquarium. Clean and disinfect it with a 5-percent bleach solution when needed. One of the great advantages of cork islands and basking areas is that, unlike rock structures, they are non-abrasive to a turtle's shell. Cork tends to be expensive, but its usefulness and attractive appearance make it well worth the money.

When kept in groups, red-eared sliders like to gather on the same basking sites. Photo by Chris Estep

Custom-made platforms are also useful waterline basking areas. Add them to the aquarium while it is bare. The best designs involve siliconing ledges or pegs onto the sides of the aquarium, allowing owners to place removable Plexiglass platforms or other easily washable segments at a level suitable for a basking area. Alternatively, you can construct a removable platform on legs and place it in the enclosure.

A hatchling peninsula cooter demonstrates a common spread-leg basking behavior performed by its species and other related turtles.

Some of the most commonly used basking areas are those that are built up from the bottom of an aquarium or plastic enclosure. The simplest types consist of a stack of bricks with a large, smooth, flat rock on top. You can also build basking areas by simply stacking smooth, flat rocks, which creates a graded access to a basking area. To prevent accidental injuries, take care that any stacked rocks are set firmly in place.

Fresh water driftwood and other kinds of wood anchored to rock or set in concrete are also used to create basking areas. If using concrete, allow it to dry then cure it for at least one week in a container of water before using it with turtles.

Give some thought to the design of the basking area(s) in your turtle vivarium. On one level, think turtle, and design easily accessible areas that will cause minimal shell abrasion and allow for plenty of swimming space. At another level, consider the aesthetic appeal of your design. Finally, create basking areas that are easy to maintain.

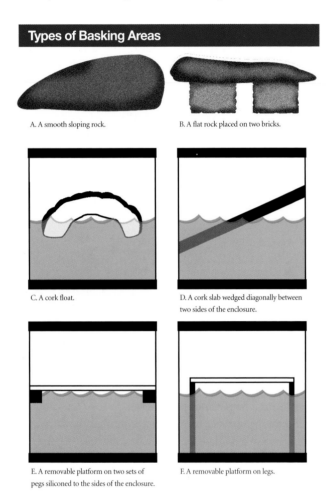

Types of Basking Areas

A. A smooth sloping rock.

B. A flat rock placed on two bricks.

C. A cork float.

D. A cork slab wedged diagonally between two sides of the enclosure.

E. A removable platform on two sets of pegs siliconed to the sides of the enclosure.

F. A removable platform on legs.

Plants

Red-eared sliders and most freshwater turtles either eat or destroy any live plants in their enclosures unless they are planted outside of the water, well outside of the reach of the turtles. However, plastic aquarium plants can be used effectively in the water section of turtle vivaria as long as their base is firmly anchored between rocks or in concrete.

Plastic plants provide small turtles with rest areas. With small turtles, certain plants, such as pothos, can be grown hydroponically in the tank, with the leaves and stems growing above water. For decorative purposes, you can set up a second tank with plants, wood, and mosses behind the turtle aquarium. It will provide an attractive, easily maintained backdrop for your vivarium, giving it a lush appearance without the hassle.

Tank and Turtle Maintenance

For the proper maintenance of your turtles, establish daily and weekly routines. Daily, perform a quick visual check of your turtles to determine their state of health. Check for swollen eyes, inactivity, injuries, shell problems, and unusual behaviors. When transferring turtles to a feeding container, examine them. Check the shell for infections and, by pressing lightly against the plastron or rear marginals, check for metabolic bone disease. Every one to two days, when the turtles are fed, monitor what they eat. Once or twice a week, siphon any excess wastes from the bottom of the enclosure. At least once a week, partially or completely change the water, examine the filtration systems, and replace the filtering media if needed. In most cases, turtle setups require fifteen to twenty minutes of mainte-

This extremely basic setup for keeping fresh-water turtles uses a large plastic tub.

nance a week. In some cases, when large setups or pools are involved, they may require up to half an hour.

Shell and Skin Shedding
Freshwater turtles regularly shed superficial cell layers of skin and occasionally shed thin, semi-transparent layers of the keratinous shell. Skin shedding in healthy turtles occurs in such thin, patchy layers that it is seldom noticed. Turtles that chronically shed large, thick sections of skin have a skin or internal disease that requires diagnosis and treatment. If a turtle chronically sheds keratinous shell scutes or the entire keratinous layers (exposing the bony shell), it probably has a shell infection or a disease that requires treatment.

Salmonellosis
Salmonellosis is a serious disease of the digestive tract and is the reason that the sale of baby turtles became illegal in the United States. During the height of the baby red-eared slider trade, several thousand cases of children stricken with salmonellosis, including a number of deaths, were directly linked to handling turtles.

To prevent the possibility of infection by *Salmonella* in the course of maintenance and handling, make sure your household obeys the following rules when handling water turtles:

1) After handling a turtle, thoroughly wash your hands with an antiseptic scrub. Do not delay. This procedure must be a standard routine. Make sure your children follow this rule.

2) Do not put your hands in your mouth while handling turtles.

3) Never kiss a turtle. Let children know that there are tiny organisms that live in turtles' water that can make them very sick.

CHAPTER 5

WATER AND FILTRATION

Providing clean water is one of the most difficult elements of turtle ownership. Turtles are usually voracious feeders and tend to be messy about it. Because they eat a lot, they also defecate a lot. That means that owners must change their water regularly. Therefore, keepers must devise a system for regular water changes and cleaning of the enclosure. If the enclosure is light and relatively sturdy, such as a plastic concrete mixing container, remove the turtles and landscape features, dump the water, clean the container, and replace the water. In most cases, however, you will need to use a siphon or water pump to empty the water from an aquarium or large enclosure. Use a hose to refill the enclosure. Many consider all of this cleaning and water maintenance to be the single biggest drawback to keeping water turtles. There are often many things one would rather do than spend fifteen to twenty minutes a week changing turtle water and cleaning out the turtle tank.

The best solution is to create systems that minimize the amount of work and time required for maintenance. The following tips will facilitate this process:

1) Children will readily get involved in your maintenance routine. It can be something parents and children do together, and it's a good way to establish relationships between children and animals. Make sure everyone involved washes their hands and arms after cleaning the tank.

2) Move your turtles to a separate container when feeding them food items that easily disintegrate. Turtles foul water during feeding because they are messy in their feeding habits. They tear prey that is too big and chew messily,

spreading food into the water. They even release food while trying to swallow. In addition, certain foods are messy. They may break up in the water, leaving small sections that will soon decompose and become lodged somewhere in the vivarium. By feeding turtles in a separate, easily cleaned container, you can prevent rapid fouling of the water. Pelleted foods and live fish small enough to be swallowed whole can usually be fed in the main enclosure with minimal fouling.

3) Whenever possible, siphon out any feces on the bottom of the enclosure.

4) Use filtration systems, which will reduce, but not eliminate, the frequency of required water changes.

Water Height

In an aquarium, red-eared sliders require a water level that allows them to swim. In the wild, they inhabit areas with water that allows for plenty of depth for swimming, so their enclosures should provide the same conditions. Keep the water level at least as deep as the length of your turtle's shell. Depending on the landscape of your aquarium, the level can be much deeper. It is essential to provide a graded access to the basking area.

Water Changes

Regularly change the water of your turtle's aquarium. If you don't have a filtered aquarium, change the water once a week as long as the turtles are fed in a separate container. Take small enclosures to a sink, wash them out, and replace the water. Do not use kitchen sinks where food is prepared or dishes and utensils are washed. Wash out the sink when you're done, first with water and detergent and then with a 5-percent bleach solution. Think hygiene and sanitation.

The most common method for changing water is to siphon it out in buckets. If the tank is near a window, you can siphon the water out the window into the garden. To start siphoning, run water into the tank through a hose and disconnect the hose from the faucet, or use a self-starting siphon. Do not use your mouth to start siphoning turtle water.

Once the container is empty, wash it out. With large containers, most keepers use one hose to add water and another to remove it during cleaning. Clean the sides of the container using a cloth containing a mild water and detergent solution, then thoroughly rinse the container. If there are or were unhealthy turtles in the tank, or if the container was unusually dirty, disinfect it with a 5-percent bleach solution and thoroughly rinse the inside.

With filtered tanks, partially change the water (25 percent or more) every one to two weeks. This will help maintain the water quality in your aquarium. Change all of the water every two to four weeks. If the filtration system is failing because it is overloaded, a complete water change and cleanup is necessary.

Remember, it takes just as much work, if not more, to keep a clean turtle enclosure as it does to keep a clean fish tank. There are no shortcuts. It's part of the package of owning water turtles. The requirements are best handled by establishing set maintenance routines and by getting members of the family involved.

These Reeve's turtles crowd together in the facilities of a large reptile distributor. The large, molded plastic pool is filtered by a pond filter, and heat is provided by an infrared bulb.

Filters

Five types of filters are effective in water turtle enclosures if you feed your turtles outside of the main tank. They are:

Canister Filters

The most effective filters for aquaria are large canister filters that fit outside of the tank. They have an outflow tube that carries the water from the tank through the filter and an inflow tube that brings the filtered water back into the aquarium. Canister filters are expensive, but, considering the savings in time and labor as well as the improved appearance of an aquarium, they are well worth the expense. The filter media must be cleaned out and replaced every one to two weeks. To conceal the filter tubing, build basking areas around it or cover it with background materials such as rock or cork bark. The powerful flow created by these filters also allows you to design attractive miniature waterfalls under the inflow tube.

Recently, submersible canister filters have become available in the aquarium trade. This type of filter usually doesn't have any tubes. Instead, the entire canister unit is

Store turtle displays are kept bare for easy maintenance. The water in this particular display is filtered by large canister filters. Thick cork slabs provide basking areas under spotlights. Photo by Chris Estep

A behind-the-scenes view of a reptile store's large freshwater turtle setup shows the filter system used to keep the water clean. Regular water changes are still necessary. Photo by Chris Estep

placed in the water. These filters are reasonably effective, but their relatively small size makes them less efficient than outside canister filters, which provide greater filtration surface and rate of flow. In addition, part of the available space in the aquarium will be taken over by the filtering unit. The two advantages of submersible canister filters are their relatively inexpensive price and their compact size, which makes them particularly suitable for smaller aquaria with smaller turtles.

The aquarium housing these hatchling mata mata turtles is filtered by a submersible canister filter.

Undergravel Filters

Undergravel filters run by powerheads can be useful for filtering turtle aquaria. They work best with large tanks containing few turtles. When using undergravel filters, feed decomposable food to your turtles in a separate container, because the undergravel filter will not be able to filter and break down large food particles. These particles must be siphoned or netted out of the tank on a regular basis. Use a 2-inch layer of a small rounded pea gravel as a gravel substrate.

Eventually, the undergravel filter will become overloaded. At this point, remove the turtles, stir up the gravel, and siphon out the resulting dirty water. Refill the tank and repeat the process three or four times. If the enclosure is particularly dirty, remove the filter and substrate, thoroughly clean and disinfect the enclosure, wash out the substrate, and redo the entire setup. Because undergravel filters are biological filters that depend on microbial action, it takes up to three weeks for the microbial flora to reach adequate levels and for the filter to become fully operational.

This 60-gallon aquarium is filtered by an undergravel filter with powerheads. The tank is heated with a submersible heater and lit with full-spectrum bulbs.

Sponge Filters

High-quality sponge filters are effective with smaller turtles if you use a high rate of air flow. Do not use small, inexpensive air pumps. Clean sponge filters frequently.

Power Filters

Power filters have a limited use in water turtle enclosures because the filters require specific water levels in order to function. The necessary height of the water may create a problem when you need to both create basking areas and leave enough above-water enclosure height to contain the animals.

Custom-made aquaria with specially designed side openings allow for the use of power filters. Otherwise, the only option is to have a large tank with an island basking area in the middle, rising above the top of the tank.

Pool filters

Pool filters are moderately effective in enclosures with water turtles. They tend to get dirty rather quickly and require regular cleaning or replacement of the filtering medium.

CHAPTER 6

HEATING AND LIGHTING

Red-eared sliders and many other water turtles need to remain in warm temperatures. Heat your turtle's enclosure using the following guidelines:

Warm Areas

If the room where the turtles are kept is relatively warm (75° F), the only heat source needed is an incandescent light or spotlight in a reflector type of fixture placed over the basking area. The area closest to the light should reach 85-88° F. Usually in an aquarium, the light also warms the water to some degree. Make sure there is no chance that the light fixture could accidentally fall into the water. Place the fixture over a screen top to eliminate this possibility. Consider overall safety and fire prevention when placing the fixture (i.e., don't get fixtures with a 60-watt bulb limit when you're using a 100-watt bulb and don't let the cord rest against the hot socket part of the fixture).

These Mississippi map turtles bask on a cork slab to warm themselves. Though not as adaptable to captive conditions as red-eared sliders, they make wonderful pets. Photo by Chris Estep

Cool Areas

If the water temperature is likely to fall below 75° F, invest in a submersible water heater. Using an aquarium thermometer, calibrate your heater to maintain the water at 78-86° F. Adjust the settings of your heater until the tank temperature remains in the proper range. Do this before you add turtles to the aquarium to prevent accidental overheating. Do not trust submersible heaters with precalibrated features. They do not always keep the temperature at the indicated setting. To avoid problems, buy an aquarium thermometer.

Because water turtles are vigorous and active animals, it is important to place submersible heaters in sheltered sections of the enclosure not readily accessible by a turtle (e.g., in the narrow space between a stacked rock basing area and the enclosure wall). Larger red-eared sliders will dislodge submersible heaters and sometimes accidentally break them.

Hatchlings

If you are raising hatchlings or young sliders and you want them to grow rapidly, raise the water temperature to 82-85° F. If fed on a regular basis, temperature will affect th growth rate of young sliders.

The Death Zone

A common cause of turtle death is an intermediate temperature zone, too warm to allow for hibernation yet too cool to stimulate hunger and allow for effective function of the immune system. For many turtles, this is a range between 66 and 72° F. Red-eared sliders kept for prolonged periods of time at these temperatures without a proper basking area stop feeding and can develop respiratory infections.

Electrical Hazards

One of the dangers of keeping water turtles is electric shock or electrocution. A spotlight accidentally falling in the water, a powerhead inadvertently submerged in water, or a broken water heater can all lead to accidental shock or electrocution. To prevent this from happening, connect all electrical appliances to a ground-fault interrupter, a device sold in many hardware stores. If an unforeseen accident occurs in your enclosure, this ten-dollar device may save your life.

Additional Lighting

When raising red-eared sliders, exposure to full-spectrum lighting is recommended, but not required, as long as an appropriate diet is provided. Nonetheless, many hobbyists choose to provide full-spectrum lighting because the ultraviolet light produced by these bulbs may have psychological benefits.

Sunlight

Experts recommend placing turtles in outdoor tubs or pools (with water and basking areas) to allow regular exposure to sunlight when possible, particularly when raising hatchlings. However, it is not a requirement for successful raising and maintenance.

A collection of red-eared sliders at a public display, shown here basking in the sun. Photo by Chris Estep

CHAPTER 7

FEEDING

A s adults, red-eared sliders are opportunistic omnivores that eat a varied diet. Feed them every two to three days. As hatchlings and juveniles, they are primarily carnivorous and grow at a significantly greater rate when raised on diets that are 25 to 40 percent protein. Offer food to hatchling and juvenile turtles on a daily basis.

Hatchling and Subadult Diets

When possible, vary the diets of hatchlings and subadults using the following foods:

Commercial Diets: Commercial diets include trout chow (Purina), floating fish diets, turtle and reptile pellets, sticks and tablets. Many of the available turtle diets have adequate nutritional values for rearing turtles and are recommended by many herpetoculturists. Try not to feed more than your turtles will eat to minimize waste and water fouling. Though many pelleted and stick diets are expensive, they are recommended as a dietary staple because they are nutritious, do not require preparation, and do not readily foul water. The author prefers pelleted foods for smaller turtles rather than floating sticks, because turtles usually swallow pellets whole and tend to break floating sticks into pieces, releasing food particles in the water. The small floating pellets used for feeding small goldfish are readily eaten and especially good for hatchling turtles.

Pre-Killed and Live Feeder Fish: Regularly offer pre-killed guppies to hatchlings, and eventually supply feeder platies and small feeder goldfish for larger turtles. An advantage to live feeder fish is that they usually fare well in the enclosure until the turtles decide to make sushi out of them. Make sure all feeder fish, live or pre-killed, are the appropriate size. Do not feed frozen fish filets or feeder fish. They may contain high levels of thiaminase and can cause a thiamin deficiency in your turtles.

Earthworms: Many turtles enjoy earthworms as part of their diet.

Select Meats: Red-eared sliders will eat lean, finely cut pieces of beef and beef heart, or cut pieces of cooked chicken (raw chicken may harbor *Salmonella*). All of these meats are calcium deficient and should be supplemented. Do not use meat exclusively. Instead, it should be one component of your turtle's diet.

Yellow-bellied sliders can be maintained using the same guidelines presented for red-eared sliders.

Dog Food: You can feed moistened, high-quality, low-fat dry dog food to hatchlings and subadults. Canned dog food, the leaner the better, is also an acceptable part of a varied turtle diet. Check the fat percentage listed at the back of the can. Trout chow and commercial diets are a much better alternative, but many people have successfully raised sliders using canned dog food as a primary component of the diet. Canned dog food quickly fouls water and leaves a film of fat on the sides of the enclosure.

Cat Food: Some keepers recommend Tender Vittles as a turtle diet, but they should only constitute part of a more varied diet.

Food Processor Diets: Food processors allow you to mince foods and make them easy to grab, tear, and swallow for turtles of all sizes. The following food processor formula makes an effective diet:
> one part commercial diet (sticks, pellets, chow)
> one part beef heart
> one part cooked chicken or fresh fish filets
> one part mixed vegetables

For each pound of this mixture, add:
> ½ teaspoon calcium/D_3 supplement
> ½ teaspoon reptile mineral/multivitamin

The components of food-processed diets can be varied depending on what's available. Finely minced diets are highly recommended with hatchlings but also work well for adults. The main problem is that they can be messy. Some herpetoculturists mix in gelatin or agar (a thickening agent) to help maintain consistency and retard the rate of disintegration.

Plant Matter: Offer romaine lettuce and other dark green lettuces to all ages of red-eared sliders, from hatchling to adult. The leaves float on the surface of the water, and turtles will nip at them as they are needed. Also offer finely chopped mixed vegetables at least once a week. As the turtles grow older, they will consume more plant matter.

Diets for Adults
Adults eat the same foods listed for subadults, but fish, commercial diets, and meat should only make up 60 percent of their diet. Adults require a variety of plant matter. In the wild, adult red-eared sliders are primarily

vegetarian. Suitable vegetable fare includes: whole leaves of romaine and red leaf lettuce, kale, swiss chard, shredded carrots, shredded squash, thawed frozen mixed vegetables, and miscellaneous cut fruit.

Vitamin and Mineral Supplements

With the proper diet, red-eared sliders do not need additional supplements. Many herpetoculturists supplement the diets of hatchlings and juveniles with a calcium/vitamin D_3 supplement. Restrict any such supplementation to no more than twice a week and only once a week as animals become older. During egg-laying season, it is a good idea to supplement the diet of gravid females once to twice a week with a calcium/vitamin D_3 supplement. Excessive calcium/vitamin D_3 supplementation can lead to abnormal shells and other problems in adults.

Calcium Blocks

You can easily make blocks of calcium carbonate by mixing plaster of Paris with water until it has a thick yet smooth consistency and pouring it to a height of a ½ inch to 1½ inches in a pie pan. Allow it to dry in a warm area for at least a week, preferably longer. When it is thoroughly dry, break it into pieces and introduce a small section into the pool or aquarium. Water turtles will nip off pieces and ingest them. If you are concerned about providing enough calcium during breeding or when raising hatchlings, use these blocks.

Gravel Ingestion

Given the opportunity, many red-eared sliders will ingest and consequently defecate large amounts of small gravel or pebbles. Some specialists feel that there are benefits to this ingestion and recommend offering small non-abrasive aquarium gravel in one area of the enclosure. Another alternative is crushed limestone sold for use in marine aquaria. If limestone is provided, it may also provide additional calcium in the diet. There are differing opinions on this subject but many aquatic turtles appear to voluntarily swallow small pebbles.

Diet and Color

As a rule, the color of red-eared sliders in captivity tends to fade. This is particularly obvious with the ornate red-eared sliders from Texas, which tend to lose their bright orange and yellow colors within a few months from capture. This loss of bright coloration, involving a fading of yellow and red pigments, is the result of insufficient plant and animal pigments in their diet.

Occasionally feed pelleted "color foods" normally used for tropical fish to help turtles maintain their bright colors. Offering a variety of plant matter high in yellow and red pigments will also contribute to maintaining brightness.

CHAPTER 8

BREEDING

According to the U.S. Food and Drug Administration (FDA), dealers cannot sell turtles under 4 inches in the United States except for scientific or educational purposes. Although this law discourages captive breeding, many herpetoculturists do not view it as an obstacle to breeding efforts and thousands of baby turtles of various species are bred, traded, and sold under various agreements throughout the United States.

Aside from large-scale commercial breeders, whose primary goals are foreign markets, the interest in captive breeding of red-eared sliders by U.S. herpetoculturists has focused on the selective breeding of desirable and valuable morphs, such as the albino red-ears and select pastels. As must be obvious, the sale and exchange of these captive-bred turtles in the United States is a rather gray legal issue, and many people walk a fine line. Remember that legally, such turtles can only be sold for export, exhibition, scientific, or educational purposes. To date, there has been

The sliders typically sold under the name "pastel" have a wide range of aberrations, including absence of pattern, abnormal scutes, and unusual color or pattern. Photo by Chris Wood

relatively little harassment of private herpetoculturists by the FDA and other regulatory agencies with regards to the trade between individuals of captive-bred baby turtles. The law appears to be aimed at large-scale commercial production of water turtles for the domestic retail pet trade, with particular emphasis on the normal red-eared sliders.

Nonetheless, the law exists and it can be enforced. So a key question you must ask before getting into breeding red-eared sliders is: What do you intend to do with the offspring? Unless you have an outlet, it may be best to avoid breeding red-eared sliders or to destroy the eggs after laying. Make responsible decisions.

Before Breeding

Breeding red-eared sliders and many other temperate water turtles is a relatively easy process. Often, captive breeding occurs without any special efforts on the part of herpetoculturists, but if your aim is consistent long-term breeding, you must give special attention to environmental conditions and proper animal management.

Before even considering breeding, make sure that:

1) You have at least one male/female pair of animals. Several pairs will yield better breeding results. If a few of the animals do not breed during breeding season, the remainder of the collection will still be able to breed (assuming the conditions were adequate).

2) The animals are sexually mature. In captivity, if your turtles were raised under optimal conditions, breeding males should be at least two and a half, preferably three and half, years old. Females reach sexual maturity at about four and half years old.

3) The animals are healthy and have good weight. Never hibernate a sick turtle.

Breeding Conditioning

The most consistent breeding results are obtained with red-eared sliders that are cooled down during the winter. Beginning in January, keep red-eared sliders at 50-60° F for a period of six to eight weeks. Do this by placing the turtle enclosure in a cool room of the house. Turn off any heating units, and cut the hours of lighting over the basking area to ten hours. Sliders usually do not feed at these colder temperatures and spend most of their time in the water section. Males will often attempt breeding with females at these colder temperatures and some herpetoculturists feel that successful breeding frequently happens during the cooling period (in contrast to many other temperate reptiles who breed after the cooling period). One view is that the sluggish behavior of the females allows for ready breeding by males.

After six to eight weeks, return the turtles to normal maintenance temperatures, and place them on an optimal feeding schedule. Egg-laying will occur from spring through summer. Some herpetoculturists keep their turtles outside during that time, in an enclosure that includes a

Malayan leaf turtles are hardy, easily maintained turtles, but they require winter temperatures above 70° F.

water area, a land area, and an egg-laying section. Use a large container with 12 to 16 inches of moistened garden soil or a moistened peat moss and soil mix. This provides an egg-laying area when female turtles are ready to lay. Other hobbyists closely monitor their turtle's behaviors. Female turtles that are nearing egg-laying typically stop feeding and become unusually active. Once this occurs, herpetoculturists remove the female turtles from the enclosure and place them in a large container with 12 to 16 inches of soil, as previously mentioned. Female turtles that are ready to lay will usually do so within one or two days.

Red-eared sliders lay several clutches of four to twenty-five (usually four to ten) eggs per breeding season. Depending on several factors, including the age and size of the turtle and the feeding and maintenance schedule, egg clutches will be laid at intervals of two to four weeks. Specialist breeders consistently obtain five to eight clutches per year from large adult red-eared sliders.

These frequent clutches are only possible when females are properly fed between clutches. High protein diets of feeder fish and commercial food sticks during the breeding season increase the potential for multiple clutches.

Incubation

Following laying, remove the eggs and place them in a container with moistened vermiculite (equal parts of vermiculite and water, by weight). Place the eggs on the surface of the vermiculite in small, finger-made depressions to prevent rolling. Mark the top of the eggs with an "X" using a magic marker to ensure that they remain in the same position. The "up" side should remain on top throughout the entire incubation. Keep the container sealed, except for a few holes for aeration, and incubate the eggs at 80-82° F. Regularly inspect the eggs, and lightly spray the vermiculite

This collection of hatchling red-eared sliders includes hypoxanthic and red pastels, and albinos.

with water to retain moisture. Hatching normally occurs in fifty-five to sixty-five days.

As with many turtles from the same family, the sex of red-eared sliders appears to be temperature-determined during the first weeks of incubation. Eggs incubated at 75° F will yield primarily females. The suggested incubation temperature should result in hatchlings of both sexes.

CHAPTER 9

DISEASES AND DISORDERS

Metabolic Bone Disease

In hatchling turtles, metabolic bone disease used to be known as soft-shell disease. It was one of the more common causes of deaths during the height of large-scale sale of baby red-eared sliders in the 1960s.

The causes of metabolic bone disease are inadequate calcium, an inadequate calcium/phosphorous ratio, and vitamin D_3 deficiency. This disease used to be common at a time when worthless turtle diets, such as dried flies, were commercially marketed in the pet trade. The earliest symptoms are the softening of the plastron and the rear marginals. When examining for metabolic bone disease, apply slight, gentle pressure to these areas. Too much force and pressure can injure the animals, so be gentle. If you follow the feeding instructions in this book, your animals will not develop metabolic bone disease. To arrest the progress of the disease, provide an adequate diet and supplement it with a calcium/phosphorous/vitamin D_3 supplement. Symptoms in larger animals include a soft shell, deformed shell growth, and the inability to stand on their hind legs. As long as the turtle still appears active and is feeding, this disease can be arrested. If caught and treated in the early stages, no long-term effects will occur. In more severe cases, the effects of the disease will not reverse and skeletal deformities and abnormal shell growth will remain for the rest of the turtle's life. In severe cases, consult a veterinarian, who will likely administer injectable calcium gluconate.

Swollen Eyes

Swollen and shut eyes are common symptoms of an inadequate diet for baby red-eared sliders. In captivity, this is often caused by vitamin A deficiency (hypovitaminosis A). If you have followed the dietary regimen suggested in this book, you should not have this problem with your turtles. Treatment involves supplementation with vitamin A, either orally or by injection. Swollen and shut eyes are also symptoms of respiratory infection and may require antibiotic therapy (see Respiratory Infections).

Internal Parasites

Red-eared sliders can harbor many parasites, including roundworms, flukes, and protozoans. If your turtle is listless, not feeding well, or has poor weight, runny or bloody stools, stools with large amounts of mucus, or stools with worms, consult a veterinarian to perform a stool check for parasites. A qualified reptile veterinarian will prescribe and perform the best treatment.

Ear or Cheek Infections

The most obvious symptom of an ear or cheek infection is an asymmetrical appearance of the head, in which one side appears more swollen than the other. Treatment involves draining the infected area through a small incision (disinfect the site of infection and the lancing tool with antiseptic scrub and alcohol). Flush the area with hydrogen peroxide and then again with antiseptic scrub. This procedure is often performed by experienced herpetoculturists, but inexperienced hobbyists should consult a veterinarian. Keep the turtle relatively dry during healing by allowing only a limited period of activity in water once a day. Upon removal from the water, disinfect the surface of the affected area with antiseptic scrub. If the infection persists, consult a veterinarian for administration of injectable antibiotics. The causes of these infections can include unsanitary or inadequate husbandry, inadequate maintenance temperature, superficial lacerations, and inadequate diet.

Shell Infections

Both fungal and bacterial organisms have been associated with the shell diseases popularly known as shell rot or shell fungus. Whatever the causes, the symptoms and treatment are similar. Symptoms include superficial ulcers of the keratinous horny shell. In time, the bony plates of the shell can be affected, resulting in varying degrees of pitting. Sometimes an infection occurs between the keratinous shell and the bony plates, resulting in a lifting of the keratinous layer. Treatment of superficial infections consists of daily application of antiseptic cream to the infected areas until the lesions have healed. In more severe cases, where the bony shell may be affected, gently clean the area and remove any infected debris before applying antiseptic scrub. In time, these lesions will gradually heal themselves. Early diagnosis is important to minimize the threat to a turtle. To prevent shell infections from occurring, it is important that you maintain your turtles in clean water without landscape structures that may damage or scrape their shells. In several species of turtles, *Beneckia chitinovora* (bacteria occurring in crawfish and shrimp) has been implicated in the outbreak and transmission of this disease. Don't feed crawfish to your turtles.

Respiratory Infections

Early symptoms of respiratory infections include runny nose, watery eyes, partially closed eyes, bubbly mucus at the edges of the mouth, and open-mouth breathing. Sick turtles also show signs of decreased appetite and inactivity. In water turtles, a frequent symptom is the inability to maintain normal equilibrium when swimming. The turtles appear to swim lopsided. Because lungs play a key role in maintaining buoyancy, when one side is congested or infected, the normal balance is lost. When both sides are affected, a turtle will constantly struggle to remain at the surface or to dive. The standard treatment is to raise the temperature to 88-94° F and to treat with antibiotics. The most effective course of treatment is to administer injectable aminoglycosides such as gentamicin or amikacin. Except in the earliest stages, when heat treatment may be effective, consult a veterinarian for safe and effective antibiotic treatment. If caught early, the prognosis is generally good.

Weight Loss, Runny Stools, or Lack of Appetite

In water turtles, weight loss, listlessness, failure to feed, and/or runny stools are usually signs of internal parasites or gastrointestinal bacterial infections. To diagnose these diseases, have a veterinarian perform a fecal exam or cloacal swab. Once diagnosed, many gastrointestinal infections are often easily treatable with parasiticides or antibiotics.

Salmonellosis

Salmonella organisms make up a significant portion of the normal intestinal flora of many turtles but, when an animal is sufficiently stressed, the bacteria can become pathogenic to the host. In turtles, symptoms include enteritis, pneumonia, mucus-covered, blood-tinged and discolored stools, runny stools, and loss of appetite. If the above symptoms are present, take the turtles to a veterinarian for a checkup and testing. Salmonellosis can be treated with injectable antibiotics. Salmonellosis can quickly spread to the rest of your collection or infect people. Take all necessary precautions to prevent spread of the disease by quarantining sick animals and routinely disinfecting hands and any tools or utensils after handling or treating sick animals.

CHAPTER 10

OTHER POPULAR FRESHWATER TURTLES

Many freshwater turtles can be maintained under conditions identical to those suitable for red-eared sliders. Tropical species need to be kept slightly warmer and should not be subjected to hibernation. Species from cool streams or colder bodies of water should be kept at cooler temperatures (e.g., big head turtles *(Platysternon megacephalum)* and loggerhead musk turtles *(Kinosternon minor))*. The following are notes on some of the more commonly sold species in the pet trade:

Painted Turtles *(Chrysemys picta)*

Painted turtles rank among the most beautiful of all freshwater turtles and make incredible display animals. Because of their size, they eventually require large tanks at least 48 inches long (standard 55-gallon aquarium). Provide deep swimming space and basking areas. A diet rich in yellow and red plant pigments (xanthophylls and carotenoids), as well as color enhancers such as canthaxanthins (found in some commercial cichlid and turtle pellets), helps these turtles preserve high color intensity.

Size: Painted turtles grow up to 10 inches long.

Sexing: Follow the same guidelines presented for red-eared sliders.

Diet: Follow the same guidelines presented for red-eared sliders.

Maintenance: Follow the same guidelines presented for red-eared sliders. Clean water is important for the long-term maintenance of these turtles. They fare best kept by themselves and not in mixed collections. When kept with other species, they are highly susceptible to several diseases, including shell infection. Keep painted turtles in water with a pH of 6.5 to reduce the likelihood of fungal infections of the shell.

Breeding: Follow the same guidelines presented for red-eared sliders. The number of eggs per clutch varies from two to twenty. Females lay two or three clutches per year. The sex of hatchlings is temperature determined; eggs incubated at 87° F result in male turtles and eggs incubated at 77° F yield mostly females. Studies show that the moisture level of the incubation substrate can affect sex determination in painted turtles.

Mississippi Map Turtles *(Graptemys kohnii)*
Overall, Mississippi map turtles are less adaptable to captivity than red-eared sliders, but they are still not difficult to keep. Larger animals may be initially reluctant to feed. This species and other members of the genus *Graptemys*

Clean and impeccable captive conditions are required for keeping any species of map turtle, such as this Mississippi map turtle. Experts also recommend full-spectrum lighting or sunlight.

are prone to shell rot, shell fungus, and skin infections.

Size: Males grow up to 5 inches and females can reach 10 inches in length.

Sexing: Males are smaller than females and have much longer tails. Adult females have larger heads.

Diet: Use the same diet listed for red-eared sliders with a greater emphasis on the carnivorous component. If a recently purchased false map turtle is reluctant to feed, offer shrimp or clams to get it started. However, do not feed these two items exclusively.

Maintenance: Mississippi map turtles can be kept like red-eared sliders. Clean water is very important to their welfare.

Breeding: Mississippi map turtles breed under the same conditions mentioned for red-eared sliders.

Softshell Turtles (*Trionychidae* spp.)

In the proper setup, softshell turtles make interesting display animals. The biggest problem with most softshell species is that they often grow too large for the typical household. As display animals, properly kept softshells will remain buried in sand a significant amount of time. Nonetheless, their intense eyes and protruding, snorkel-like snout are hard to resist.

Size: Softshells are large turtles. U.S. species commonly sold in the pet trade can range from 5 inches (small males) to 18 inches (large female western spiny softshells). The largest U.S. softshell is the Florida softshell turtle. Females can reach a length of 2 feet and will eventually require an enclosure at least the size of a small pool.

Sexing: Males are smaller with longer tales.

Diet: Softshell turtles are carnivorous. Feed them appropriately sized feeder fish, pre-killed mice, high-quality dog food (both canned or soaked dry), beef heart, and commercial pelleted or stick diets.

Maintenance: Clean water is essential for softshell turtles. The bottom of the enclosure should have a layer of fine, smooth, rounded sand deep enough for the turtles to bury in. Biologically active silt collected from the bottom of a clean pond or stream works best. Some herpetoculturists have had success at keeping softshell turtles in relatively bare containers with no substrate, as long as clean, high-quality water is provided. The ability to adapt to such conditions varies from species to species and from individual to individual. Use a canister filter in softshell enclosures, not an undergravel filter. Do not place abrasive rocks or surfaces in the landscape. All basking areas should be smooth, such as smooth rocks, weathered wood, or Plexiglass platforms.

Proper maintenance temperatures depend on the animals' native habitat. Species from the United States can be maintained at the same temperatures as red-eared sliders. Tropical species, including the Asian species regularly imported for the pet trade, require temperatures ranging from 82-86° F.

Breeding: For American species, use pre-breeding conditions and incubation techniques similar to those listed for red-eared sliders. For pre-breeding conditioning of tropical species, reduce the temperature to the mid 70s F for four to eight weeks.

Handling: Do not handle your softshell turtles. All species tend to bite and do not like handling.

Additional Selection Tips: In addition to criteria mentioned for red-eared sliders, pay careful attention to avoid turtles with sores on the shell or body.

Additional Medical Concerns: Gastroenteritis is common

in Asian species. In all softshells, septicemic cutaneous ulcerative disease, known as SCUD, is common, particularly when the proper substrate is absent. This skin and shell disease, characterized by large ulcers on the underside of the limbs and shell, is often undiagnosed until it has progressed to more advanced stages. Though patients with SCUD will respond to several antibiotics, including chloramphenicol, gentamicin, and amikacin, prognosis is questionable and partially depends on how early treatment was initiated. A suitable substrate must be supplied following treatment. Biologically active substrates, such as fine sand or silt, have proven beneficial to softshell turtle maintenance. Using a layer of silt collected from the bottom of a clean pond or stream as the substrate of a softshell enclosure can prevent SCUD from appearing in captive collections. Replace the silt regularly, every two to three months.

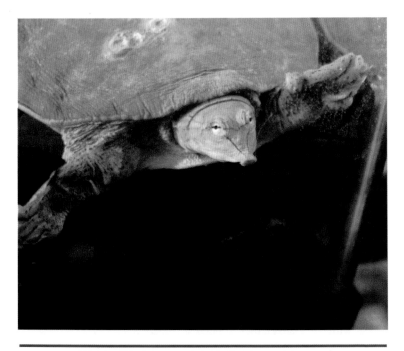

The sores on the carapace of this spiny softshell turtle were not caused by septicemic cutaneous ulcerative disease (SCUD). Treatment with antiseptic scrub will probably take care of the problem.

Musk and Mud Turtles (*Kinosternon* spp.)

Overall, musk and mud turtles are a neglected and under-appreciated group. In an aquarium with filtered water and rocks rising near the surface, musk and mud turtles make a nifty and entertaining display. They may not be beautiful, but they have a variety of fascinating behaviors. It's true that they may bite and you can't kiss them good night, but water turtles shouldn't be handled anyway. Live plants and artificial plants can add considerably to their vivarium. If you have a chance to obtain babies of these species, you're in for a treat. These tiny turtles, which are possibly the ultimate miniature turtles, can make some of the finest display animals.

When kept under proper conditions, musk turtles, like this razor-backed musk turtle, fare well in captivity. Photo by Chris Estep

Size: Most U.S. mud and musk turtles achieve an adult size between 3 and 5 inches. The largest is the Big Bend mud turtle *(Kinosternon hirtipes murrayi)*, which can grow to slightly more than 6 inches. Tropical musk turtles are also in the same general size range. Their small size makes this group particularly amenable to indoor keeping in nicely designed aquaria.

51

Big-headed turtles, found in Southeast Asia, fare best in cool temperatures in the 70s F. They are generally hardy and aggressive with lots of personality, and can be kept like musk turtles.

Sexing: Males have longer tails than females. In some species, such as loggerhead musk turtles *(Kinosternon minor minor)*, mature males also have larger heads.

Diet: Mud and musk turtles are primarily carnivorous, but some species will feed on plant matter, such as melon and tomatoes.

Maintenance: Follow the same guidelines presented for red-eared sliders.

Snapping turtles can be maintained under the same conditions as musk and mud turtles. As with all turtles, captives should never be released in the wild. Photo by Chris Estep

Breeding: Breeding musk and mud turtles is similar to breeding red-eared sliders, except for subtropical species, which should not be cooled more than 10 degrees below the normal maintenance temperature. Most species lay one to nine eggs per clutch. Up to four clutches may be laid during the breeding season.

Reeve's Turtles *(Chinemys reevesi)*

These Asian turtles are not particularly attractive, but they have their own special appeal. In general, Reeve's turtles don't get too big (usually under 6 inches), are very hardy as captives, and, in time, show a degree of responsiveness and personality. In a nicely designed vivarium, they make interesting display animals. It is a good idea to only keep similar sized animals together, because smaller animals may be bullied and bitten by larger ones. Males may also sometimes fight with each other. Most imports are shipped out of Hong Kong.

Size: Reeve's turtles grow up to 8 inches in length, but most captives and imports range from 4 to 6 inches.

Sexing: Males have a longer tail than females, and their vent is located at a greater distance from the body. Reeve's turtles can be sexed at 2½ inches.

Diet: This species is primarily carnivorous and readily feeds on commercial turtle or cichlid pellets.

Maintenance: Follow the same guidelines presented for red-eared sliders.

Breeding: Follow the same guidelines presented for red-eared sliders. Females lay up to three clutches of four to nine eggs.

Additional Color Morphs: There are color variations in the populations of Reeve's turtles. Some populations tend toward melanism. Occasionally, unusually light specimens

are misrepresented as albinos. If the pupils do not appear orange or reddish and the animal doesn't show obvious lack of pigmentation, it is just a "light phase" or hypomelanistic Reeve's. Many people have been cheated into buying false albino Reeve's turtles.

African Sidenecked Turtles (*Pelomedusa subrufa* and *Pelusios* sp.).

In recent years, *Pelomedusa subrufa* and *Pelusios* sp. have been imported for the pet trade. The helmeted sideneck (*Pelomedusa subrufa*) is not particularly colorful, but its eyes are bright and intense. They make up for their drab appearance with lots of personality and hardiness. They are one of the hardiest types of water turtle. Imported *Pelusios* species can be kept like *Pelomedusa*, but they are more shy and less spunky than *Pelomedusa*.

Size: These species range from 6 to 10 inches in length.

Sexing: Males have a concave plastron and longer tails than females.

African helmeted sideneck turtles are a very hardy and entertaining species.

Diet: Helmeted turtles are opportunistic carnivores that will feed on a variety of live foods, meats, fish, and commercial diets.

Maintenance: Helmeted turtles have basically the same care requirements as red-eared sliders, except that winter temperatures should remain above 68° F. Expose them to cooler temperatures (the upper 80s to low 70s F) and a reduced photoperiod for four to six weeks during the winter for pre-breeding conditioning. During this cooling period, you can keep these animals on soil with just a small container of water.

Breeding: Follow the same guidelines presented for red-eared sliders. Females lay a single clutch of thirteen to forty-two eggs each season.

Mixed Collections

Generally, keeping a mixed collection of turtle species in the same enclosure is not a good idea. Mixing turtle species can expose animals to diseases and parasites to which they

Painted turtles, such as this southern painted turtle, do not fare well in mixed collections.

have little resistance. For example, mixing red-eared sliders and painted turtles often results in sickness or shell problems for the painted turtles.

CHAPTER 11

IF YOU GET TIRED OF YOUR TURTLES

Various factors lead people to get rid of their turtles, ranging from boredom to lack of time. What should they do? To start with, consider what not to do. Never release your pet turtle in the local pond, lake, or river. This practice should be (and usually is) illegal. Released red-eared sliders can displace native species and there is a chance that diseases that they harbor may harm native species. So remember: Never release a captive reptile in the wild.

When you can no longer keep a turtle, first investigate whether a friend might be interested. Another option is to take the animal to the store you bought it from and ask whether they might be interested in purchasing it back from you. Most stores will pay a wholesale price that allows them to resell the animal at a profit. You can also contact a local herpetological society and ask if they have an adoption committee that could find a good home for your animals. Whatever you do, do not release your turtle. Do not be irresponsible.

RESOURCES

Ernst, C.H. and R.W. Barbour. 1989. *Turtles of the World*. Smithsonian Institution Press.

Frye, F.L. 1981. *Biomedical and Surgical Aspects of Captive Reptile Husbandry*. Krieger Publishing: Melbourne, Fl.

Gibbons, J.W. 1990. *Life History and Ecology of the Slider Turtle*. Smithsonian Institution Press.

Zimmerman, E. 1983. *Breeding Terrarium Animals*. T.F.H.

INDEX

ABOUT THE AUTHOR

Philippe de Vosjoli is the highly acclaimed author of the best-selling reptile-care books, The Herpetocultural Library Series. His work in the field of herpetoculture has been recognized nationally and internationally for establishing high standards for amphibian and reptile care. His books, articles, and other writings have been praised and recommended by numerous herpetological societies, veterinarians, and other experts in the field. Philippe de Vosjoli was also the cofounder and president of The American Federation of Herpetoculturists, and was given the Josef Laszlo Memorial Award in 1995 for excellence in herpetoculture and his contribution to the advancement of the field.